This edition published 1995 by Geddes & Grosset Ltd,
David Dale House, New Lanark, Scotland

Illustrated by Lyndsay Duff in the style of Charles Robinson

ISBN 1 85534 530 7

Printed in Slovenia

Cock-a-doodle--do

Mother Goose Rhymes

Cock-a-doodle--do

COCK-A-DOODLE-DO

Cock-a-doodle-do!
My dame has lost her shoe;
My master's lost his fiddle-stick,
And don't know what to do.

Cock-a-doodle-do!
What is my dame to do?
Till master finds his fiddle-stick,
She'll dance without her shoe.

JOHN COOK'S GREY MARE

JOHN COOK had a little grey mare; he, haw, hum!
Her back stood up, and her bones they were bare; he, haw, hum!

John Cook was riding up Shuter's bank; he, haw, hum!
And there his nag did kick and prank; he, haw, hum!

John Cook was riding up Shuter's hill; he, haw, hum!
His mare fell down, and she made her will; he, haw, hum!

The bridle and saddle were laid on the shelf; he, haw, hum!
If you want any more you may sing it yourself; he, haw, hum!

BUZ AND HUM

UZ, quoth the blue
fly,

Hum, quoth the
bee,

Buz and hum they
cry,

And so do we.

In his ear, in his nose,
Thus, do you see?
He ate the dormouse,
Else it was he.

TOMMY
TITTLEMOUSE

Little Tommy Tittlemouse
Lived in a little house;
He caught fishes
In other men's ditches.

A AND B AND SEE

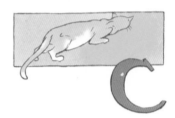

Great A, little a, bounc-
　　ing B,

The cat's in the cup-
　　board and she can't
　　see.

DOCTOR FOSTER

OCTOR Foster went
　　to Glo'ster,

In a shower of
　　rain;

He stepped in a puddle right up to his middle,
And never went there again.

DAFFY·DOWN·DILLY·

Daffy-down-dilly has come to town,

In a yellow petticoat, and a green gown.

HO MY KITTEN

HO my kitten, a kitten,
 And ho! my kitten, my deary!
Such a sweet pet as this
 Was neither far nor neary.

Here we go up, up, up,
 Here we go down, down, down;
Here we go backwards and forwards,
 And here we go round, round, round.

LAVENDER BLUE

LAVENDER blue and rosemary green,
When I am king you shall be queen;
Call up my maids at four o'clock,
Some to the wheel and some to the
  rock,
Some to make hay and some to shear
  corn,
And you and I will keep ourselves warm.

The QUARRELSOME KITTENS

TWO little kittens one stormy
night,
They began to quarrel and
they began to fight;
One had a mouse and the
other had none,
And that's the way the quarrel begun.

"I'll have that mouse," said the biggest cat.
"You'll have that mouse? we'll see about that!"
"I will have that mouse," said the eldest son.
"You sha'n't have the mouse," said the little one.

I told you before 't was a stormy night
When these two little kittens began to fight;
The old woman seized her sweeping broom,
And swept the two kittens right out of the room.

The Quarrelsome Kittens

The ground was covered with frost and snow,
And the two little kittens had nowhere to go;
So they laid them down on the mat at the door,
While the old woman finished sweeping the floor.

Then they crept in, as quiet as mice,
All wet with the snow, and as cold as ice,
For they found it was better, that stormy night,
To lie down and sleep than to quarrel and fight.

THE FLY AND THE HUMBLE-BEE

IDDLE-DE-DEE, fiddle-de-dee,
The fly shall marry the humble-bee;

They went to church and married was she,
The fly has married the humble-bee.

CAT AND DOG

Pussy sits beside the fire,
How can she be fair?
In comes the little dog,
"Pussy, are you
there?

So, so, Mistress Pussy,
Pray, how do you
do?"
"Thank you, thank
you, little dog,
I 'm very well just
now."

BOBBY SHAFT

Bobby Shaft is gone to sea,
With silver buckles at his knee;
When he'll come home he'll marry me,
Pretty Bobby Shaft!

Bobby Shaft is fat and fair,
Combing down his yellow hair;
He's my love for evermore!
Pretty Bobby Shaft!

THE LITTLE CLOCK

There 's a neat little clock,
  In the schoolroom it stands,
And it points to the time
  With its two little hands.
And may we, like the clock,
  Keep a face clean and bright,
With hands ever ready
  To do what is right.

LITTLE MAID

" Little maid, pretty maid,
    whither goest thou?"

" Down in the forest to milk
    my cow."

" Shall I go with thee?" " No,
    not now;

When I send for thee, then
    come thou."

Bat, bat,
  Come under my hat,
And I 'll give you a slice
    of bacon;

And when I bake,
  I 'll give you a cake,
If I am not mistaken.

CHRISTMAS

Christmas is coming, the geese are
  getting fat,

Please to put a penny in an old
  man's hat;

If you have n't got a penny, a ha'-
  penny will do,

If you have n't got a ha'penny, God
  bless you.

PETER WHITE

Peter White will ne'er go
  right,

  And would you know the
    reason why?

He follows his nose where'er
  he goes,

  And that stands all awry.

SLEEP·BABY·SLEEP·

LEEP, baby, sleep,
Our cottage vale is
   deep;
The little lamb is on the green,
With woolly fleece so soft
   and clean—
   Sleep, baby, sleep!

Sleep, baby, sleep,
Down where the wood-
   bines creep;
Be always like the lamb so mild,
A kind, and sweet, and gentle
   child—
   Sleep, baby, sleep!

UP PIPPEN HILL

As I was going up Pippen
Hill,
    Pippen Hill was dirty;
There I met a pretty miss,
    And she dropped me a
    curtsey.

Little miss, pretty miss,
    Blessings light upon you!
If I had half a crown a day,
    I'd spend it all upon you.

A FALLING OUT

LITTLE old man and I
    fell out;
    How shall we bring
    this matter about?
Bring it about as
    well as you can;
Get you gone, you
    little old man.

THE NUT-TREE

I HAD a little nut-tree, nothing would it bear

But a silver nutmeg and a golden pear;

The King of Spain's daughter came to see me,

And all was because of my little nut-tree.

I skipped over water, I danced over sea,

And all the birds in the air couldn't catch me.

POLLY FLINDERS

LITTLE Polly Flinders

Sat among the cinders,

Warming her ten little toes!

Her mother came and caught her,

And whipped her little daughter,

For spoiling her nice new clothes.

BRIAN O'LIN

Brian O'Lin had no breeches to wear,
So he bought him a sheep-skin and made him a pair,
With the skinny side out, and the woolly side in,
"Ah, ha, that is warm!" said Brian O'Lin.

Brian O'Lin and his wife and wife's mother,
They all went over a bridge together;
The bridge was broken and they all fell in,
"Mischief take all!" quoth Brian O'Lin.

MARGERY DAW

SEE-SAW, MARGERY DAW,

Jacky shall have a new master.

He shall have but a penny a day,

Because he can't work any faster.

NONSENSE

We are all in the dumps,
For diamonds are trumps,
    The kittens are gone to St. Paul's,
The babies are bit,
The moon's in a fit,
    And the houses are built without walls.

ANOTHER FALLING OUT

MY little old man and I fell out;

I'll tell you what 't was all about:

I had money and he had none,

And that's the way the noise begun.

Little BOY BLUE

L ITTLE BOY BLUE, come, blow up your horn;
The sheep's in the meadow, the cow's in the corn.
Where's the little boy that looks after the sheep?
Under the haystack, fast asleep.

LITTLE TOM TUCKER

Little Tom Tucker sings for his supper.

What shall he eat? White bread and butter.

How will he cut it without e'er a knife?

How will he be married without e'er a wife?

OLD WOMAN, OLD WOMAN

"OLD woman, old woman, shall we go a-shearing?"

"Speak a little louder, sir, I'm very thick of hearing."

"Old woman, old woman, shall I kiss you dearly?"

"Thank you, kind sir, I hear you very clearly."

UP HILL AND DOWN DALE

Up hill and down dale;
Butter is made in every vale;
And if that Nancy Cook
Is a good girl,
She shall have a spouse,
And make butter anon,
Before her old grandmother
Grows a young man.

LUCY LOCKET

Lucy Locket
Lost her pocket,
Kitty Fisher
Found it;
Nothing in it,
Nothing in it,
But the binding
Round it.

FORTUNE-TELLING BY DAISY PETALS

He loves me, he don't!
He'll have me, he won't!

He would if he could,
But he can't, so he don't!

A was an apple pie

B bit it,

C cut it,

D dealt it,

E eat it,

F fought for it,

G got it,

H had it,

J joined it,

K kept it,

L longed for it,

M mourned for it,